DRAW KAWAII
CUTE
ANIMALS
Step-by-step

By Isobel Lundie

BOOK HOUSE
a SALARIYA imprint

Author and illustrator:
Isobel Lundie graduated from
Kingston University in 2015
where she studied illustration and
animation. She is interested in how
colourful and distinctive artwork
can transform stories for children.

PAPER FROM

**SUSTAINABLE
FORESTS**

Published in Great Britain in MMXX by
Book House, an imprint of
The Salariya Book Company Ltd
25 Marlborough Place,
Brighton BN1 1UB
www.salariya.com

PB ISBN: 978-1-912904-41-9

SCRIBO BOOK HOUSE SCRIBBLERS

1 3 5 7 9 8 6 4 2

A CIP catalogue record for this
book is available
from the British Library.

Printed and bound in China.

Visit
www.salariya.com
for our online catalogue and
free fun stuff.

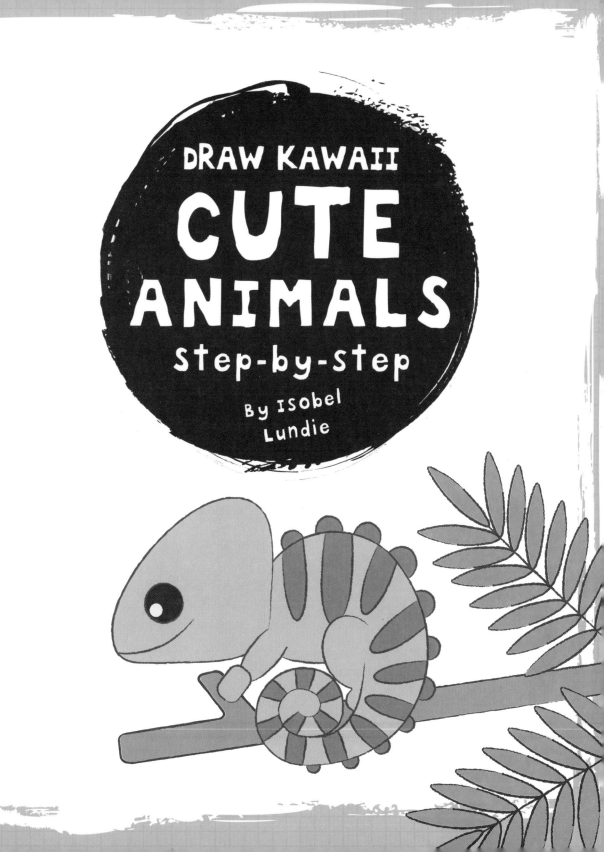

DRAW KAWAII
CUTE
ANIMALS
Step-by-step

By Isobel
Lundie

contents

introduction
what is kawaii?

Kawaii means 'cute' in the Japanese language but a Japanese art style has evolved which is also known as 'kawaii'. This style emphasises the 'cuteness' of the characters it depicts.

This book shows you how to master the techniques required to draw your own 'kawaii' animal pictures. It includes tips and general information before you start and then a series of step-by-step projects for you to follow.

Materials

Pencil
Drawing with an HB pencil makes it easy to erase any unwanted excess lines.

Materials
The ideas in this book can be done in different ways and with different materials. Here are some suggestions.

coloured paper
Try drawing kawaii animals on coloured paper!

coloured pencils
Coloured pencils are ideal for shading. See this cat drawing.

Labels

Make your own kawaii labels for your presents.

Ink

Use a small brush to make cute inky paintings!

Stickers

Draw onto stickers to make cute drawings for your friends!

Sketchbook

Use a sketchbook so you can keep all your drawings together.

Making everything cute

soften shapes
Rounding off the points of a triangle softens its shape. Try softening the edges of shapes when drawing your kawaii characters.

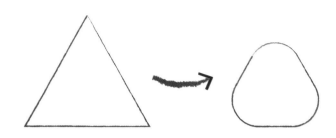

Simplify drawings
Make your drawing cuter by simplifying it down to its key features. This way you can make almost anything cute!

Proportions
The kawaii body should be proportioned as shown. A large head, with a short body and short legs.

Add a cute face

You can make almost anything cute by drawing an appealing cartoon face on it.

colours to soften

Pastel colours are cuter. Try using soft pastel colours to make your characters cuter.

Motion lines

Adding motion lines in this way is a simple and effective way to convey movement in a drawing.

Adding features

cute feet

Adding adorable feet to your characters is a good way
to make them look even cuter.

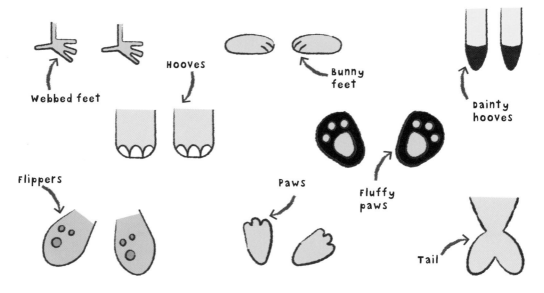

Webbed feet

Hooves

Bunny feet

Dainty hooves

Flippers

Paws

Fluffy paws

Tail

cute stuff

Don't forget that objects can help to bring a character to life!

Fish

carrot

Ball of string

Acorn

Bamboo stick

cute features

Animals have all manner of distinguishing features, from fluffy ears to beaks!
You'll need to get to know them all in order to draw them.

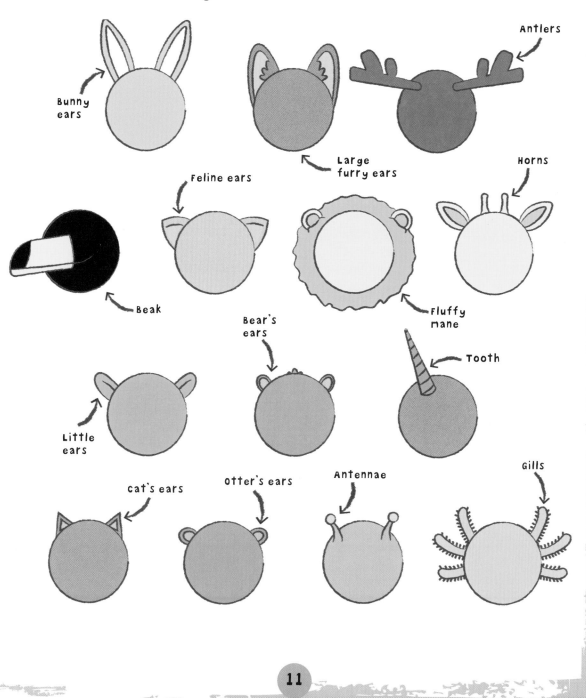

Bunny ears

Antlers

Large furry ears

Feline ears

Horns

Beak

Fluffy mane

Bear's ears

Tooth

Little ears

cat's ears

otter's ears

Antennae

Gills

Expressions

changing your character's expression adds personality.

Happy

Draw happy 'U'-shaped eyes.

Sad

Draw curved eyebrows.

Angry

Draw diagonal eyebrows.

confused

Draw one eyebrow raised.

Scared

Raise both eyebrows.

Excited

Draw the mouth wider.

crying

Draw in flowing tears.

Tired

Draw the eyes closed.

Embarrassed

Draw a pursed mouth.

Mixed-up animals

can you use the features on the previous page
to create your own mixed-up animal faces?

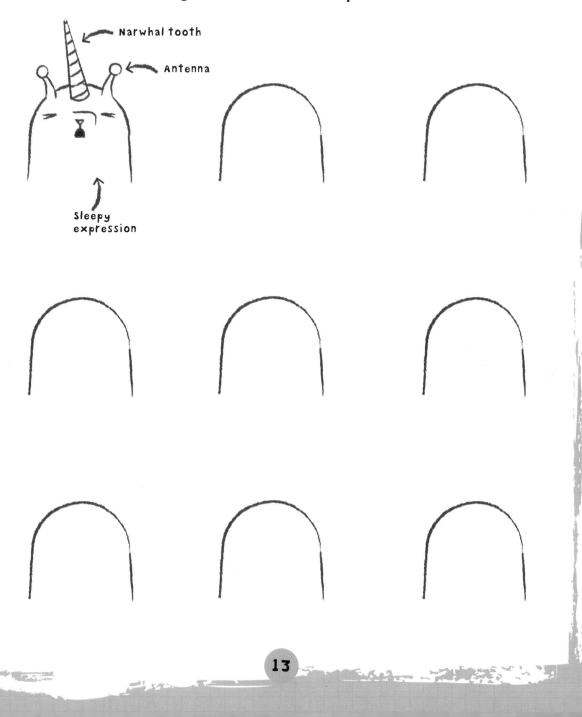

Narwhal tooth

Antenna

Sleepy
expression

Now it's your turn

Kawaii hippo

1

Ears

Body

Head

Legs

2

Draw in his eyes, nose and ears.

Add his tail.

Draw in his toenails.

3

colour him in!

1

Head

Ears

Body

Legs

2

Draw in his eyes, nose and ears.

Draw in his toenails.

3

colour him in!

Erase all unwanted construction lines.

Why not draw your kawaii hippo splashing about in a lake to keep cool?

Draw your
own hippo.

Kawaii chameleon

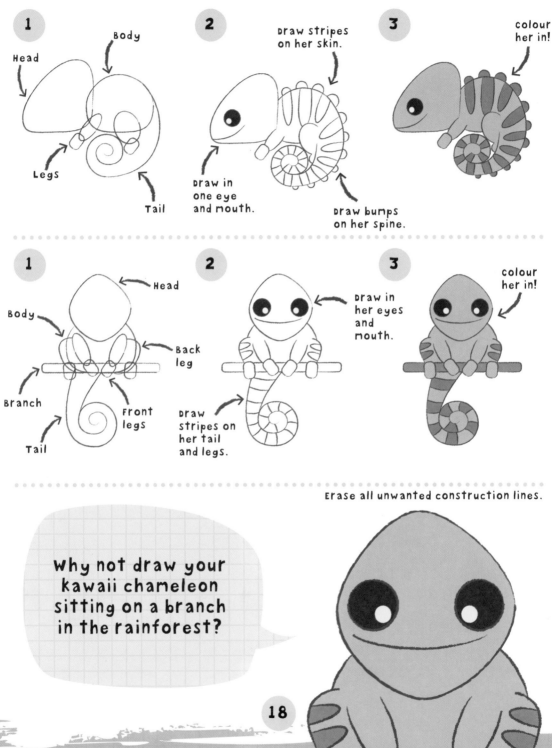

1
Head
Body
Legs
Tail

2
Draw stripes on her skin.
Draw in one eye and mouth.
Draw bumps on her spine.

3
colour her in!

1
Head
Body
Back leg
Branch
Front legs
Tail

2
Draw in her eyes and mouth.
Draw stripes on her tail and legs.

3
colour her in!

Erase all unwanted construction lines.

Why not draw your kawaii chameleon sitting on a branch in the rainforest?

18

Draw your own
chameleon.

Kawaii moose

1

Antlers   Ears

Neck

Tail

Head

Body

Legs

2 Finish drawing his antlers and ears.

Draw in eyes and nostrils.

Draw in some thick hair.

3

colour him in!

1

Ears

Head

Antlers

Neck

Tail

Body

Legs

2 Finish drawing his antlers and ears.

Draw in eyes and nostrils.

Draw in some thick hair.

3

colour him in!

Erase all unwanted construction lines.

Why not draw your kawaii moose wandering through a snowy landscape?

20

Draw your own moose.

Kawaii bat

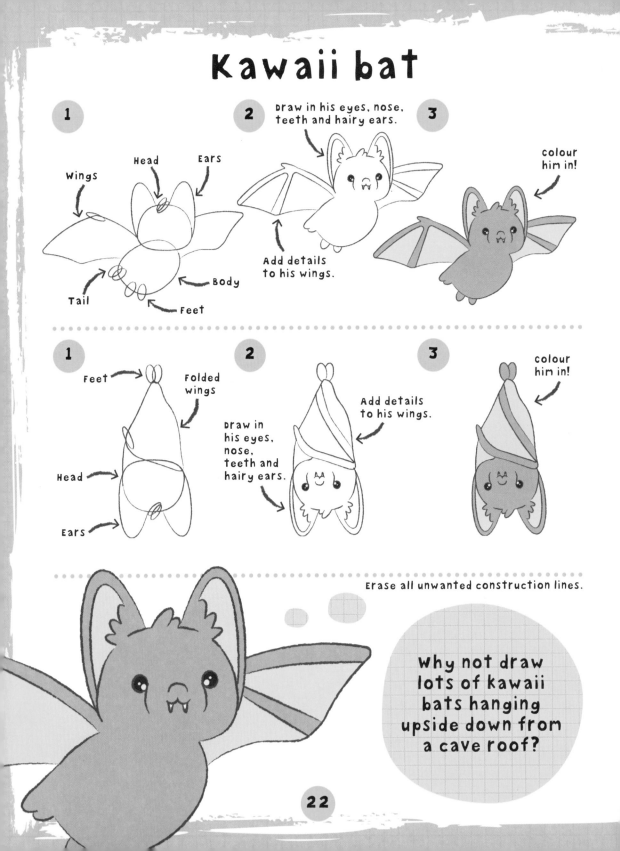

1

Wings

Head

Ears

Tail

Body

Feet

2 Draw in his eyes, nose, teeth and hairy ears.

Add details to his wings.

3 colour him in!

1

Feet

Folded wings

Head

Ears

2 Draw in his eyes, nose, teeth and hairy ears.

Add details to his wings.

3 colour him in!

Erase all unwanted construction lines.

Why not draw lots of kawaii bats hanging upside down from a cave roof?

Draw your
own bat.

Kawaii rabbit

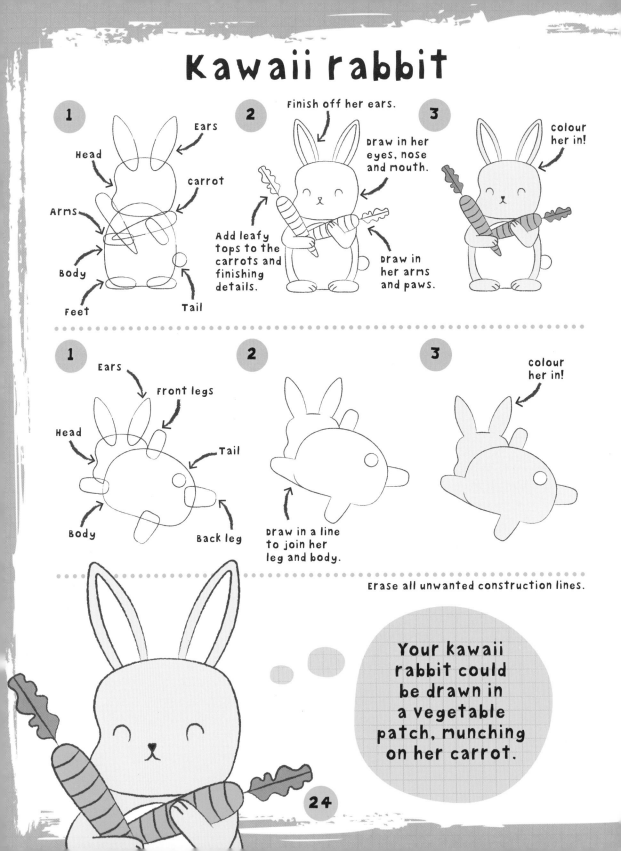

1
Head
Ears
carrot
Arms
Body
Feet
Tail

2
Finish off her ears.
Draw in her eyes, nose and mouth.
Add leafy tops to the carrots and finishing details.
Draw in her arms and paws.

3
colour her in!

1
Ears
Front legs
Head
Tail
Body
Back leg

2
Draw in a line to join her leg and body.

3
colour her in!

Erase all unwanted construction lines.

Your kawaii rabbit could be drawn in a vegetable patch, munching on her carrot.

Draw your
own rabbit.

Kawaii toucan

1
Beak
Body
Tail
Feet

2 Draw in an eye and add detail to her beak.
Draw in stripes.

3
colour her in!

1
Beak
Wings
Body
Tail
Feet

2 Draw in an eye and add detail to her beak.
Draw in stripes.

3
colour her in!

Erase all unwanted construction lines.

Why not draw your kawaii toucan flying through the rainforest?

Draw your
own toucan.

Kawaii leopard

1

Head

Ears

Tail

Back legs

Front legs

2 Draw in her eyes, nose, mouth and whiskers.

Draw in her leopard spots.

Draw in her tummy.

3

colour her in!

1

Head

Ears

Body

Tail

Front legs

Back legs

2 Draw in her leopard spots.

Draw in her eyes, nose, mouth and whiskers.

Draw in her tummy.

3

colour her in!

Erase all unwanted construction lines.

Why not draw your kawaii leopard sitting high up on a tree branch?

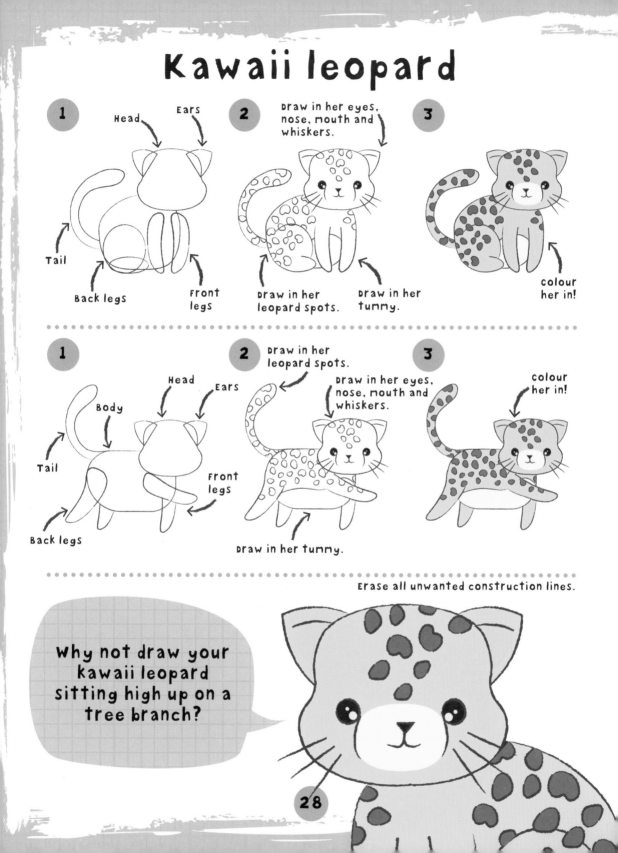

Draw your
own leopard.

Kawaii panda

1 Ears · Head · Arms · Feet · Bamboo stick

2 Draw in his nose, mouth and eye patches. · Add details to the bamboo. · Add pads to his feet.

3 colour him in!

1 Body · Ears · Tail · Head · Arms · Back leg

2 Draw in his nose, mouth and eye patches. · Draw in his black fur.

3 colour him in!

Erase all unwanted construction lines.

Why not draw your kawaii panda munching his bamboo in a forest?

30

Draw your own panda.

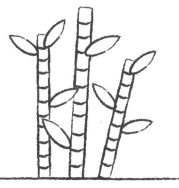

Kawaii raccoon

1

Head
Ears
Arms
Feet
Tail

2

Draw his nose, mouth, eyes and eye patches.

Draw in his ears.

Draw in his hands, tummy and back legs.

Add stripes to his tail.

3

colour him in!

1

Head
Ears
Front leg
Back leg
Body
Tail

2

Draw his nose, mouth, eyes and eye patches.

Draw in his ears.

Draw in his hand and fruit.

Add stripes to his tail.

3

colour him in!

Erase all unwanted construction lines.

Why not draw your kawaii raccoon hunting for food?

Draw your
own raccoon.

Kawaii fox

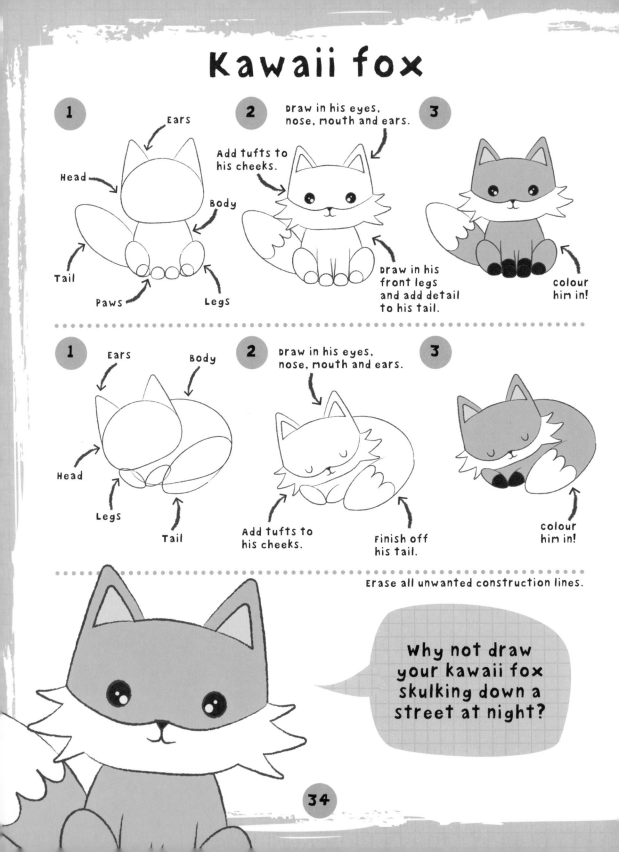

1
Ears
Head
Body
Tail
Paws
Legs

2 Draw in his eyes, nose, mouth and ears.
Add tufts to his cheeks.
Draw in his front legs and add detail to his tail.

3
colour him in!

1
Ears
Body
Head
Legs
Tail

2 Draw in his eyes, nose, mouth and ears.
Add tufts to his cheeks.
Finish off his tail.

3
colour him in!

Erase all unwanted construction lines.

Why not draw your kawaii fox skulking down a street at night?

Draw your
own fox.

Kawaii octopus

1 Body

Draw in her eyes, cheeks and mouth.

2 Add spots.

3 colour her in!

Eight arms

---

1 Body

Eight arms

2 Draw in her eyes, mouth and cheeks.

Add suckers to her arms.

3 colour her in!

Erase all unwanted construction lines.

Why not draw your kawaii octopus floating through an underwater landscape?

Draw your
own octopus.

Kawaii cat

1 Tail · Ears · Head · Body · Legs · Paws · Ball of wool

2 Draw in her eyes, nose, ears and mouth. · Add whiskers. · Add detail.

3 colour her in!

1 Head · Ears · Body · Legs · Tail

2 Draw in her eyes, nose, mouth and ears. · Add whiskers.

3 colour her in!

Erase all unwanted construction lines.

Why not draw your kawaii cat playing with her ball of wool or chasing a mouse?

Draw your own cat.

Kawaii lion

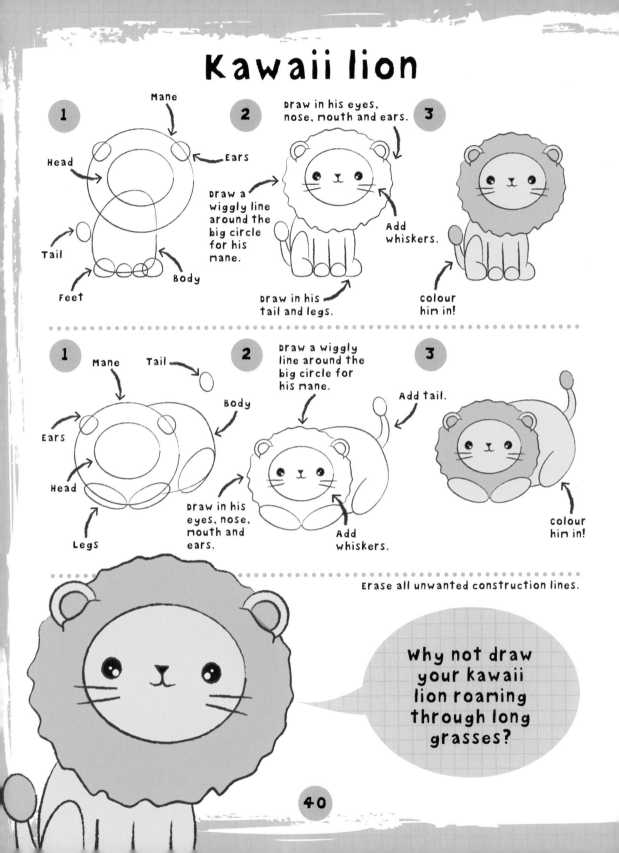

1

Mane

Head

Tail

Feet

Ears

Body

2

Draw in his eyes,
nose, mouth and ears.

Draw a
wiggly line
around the
big circle
for his
mane.

Add
whiskers.

Draw in his
tail and legs.

3

colour
him in!

1

Mane

Tail

Body

Ears

Head

Legs

2

Draw a wiggly
line around the
big circle for
his mane.

Draw in his
eyes, nose,
mouth and
ears.

Add
whiskers.

3

Add tail.

colour
him in!

Erase all unwanted construction lines.

Why not draw
your kawaii
lion roaming
through long
grasses?

40

Draw your
own lion.

Kawaii giraffe

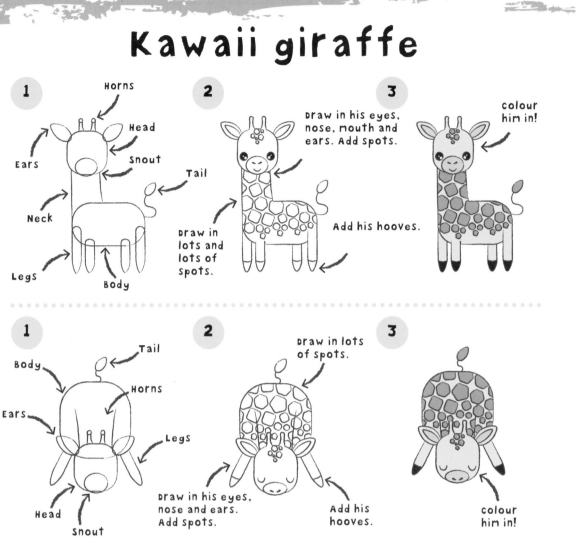

1

Horns

Head

Snout

Ears

Tail

Neck

Legs

Body

2

Draw in his eyes, nose, mouth and ears. Add spots.

Draw in lots and lots of spots.

Add his hooves.

3

colour him in!

1

Tail

Body

Horns

Ears

Legs

Head

Snout

2

Draw in lots of spots.

Draw in his eyes, nose and ears. Add spots.

Add his hooves.

3

colour him in!

Erase all unwanted construction lines.

Why not draw your kawaii giraffe stretching up to eat leaves from a tall tree?

Draw your own giraffe.

Kawaii turtle

1

Head

Tail

Flippers   Shell

2

Draw in his eyes and mouth.

Draw spots on his face and flippers.

Draw in the pattern of his shell.

3

colour him in!

1

Head

Shell

Tail

Draw in spots on his face and flippers.

Flippers

2

Draw in his eyes and mouth.

Draw in the pattern of his shell.

3

colour him in!

Erase all unwanted construction lines.

Why not draw your kawaii turtle swimming through the ocean?

44

Draw your
own turtle.

Kawaii narwhal

1 Head

Tail Body Fins

2 Draw in his eyes, mouth and tooth.

Add three spots.

Draw his tummy.

3 colour him in!

1 Body

Tail

Fins

Draw in his eyes, mouth and tooth.

2 Add three spots.

Draw his tummy.

3 colour him in!

Erase all unwanted construction lines.

Why not draw your kawaii narwhal swimming up to the surface of the ocean?

46

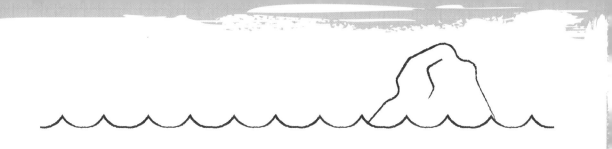

Draw your
own narwhal.

Kawaii hamster

1

Tuft of fur
Ears
Head
cheeks
Arms
Feet
Body

2

Draw in his eyes, nose, ears, mouth and teeth.

Draw in his tummy.

3

colour him in!

1

Ears
Tuft of fur
Body
cheeks
Feet
Head
Back leg
Tail

2

Draw in his eyes, nose, ears, mouth and teeth.

3

colour him in!

Erase all unwanted construction lines.

Why not draw your kawaii hamster running round and round in his hamster wheel?

48

Draw your
own hamster.

Kawaii Seal

1
Head
Body
Flippers
Tail
Flippers

2
Draw in his eyes, nose, mouth and whiskers.
Add a tuft of fur.
Draw spots on his back.
Flippers

3
colour him in!

1
Head
Fish
Flippers
Fish tail
Body
Tail
Flippers

2
Add a tuft of fur.
Add details to the fish.
Draw in his eyes, nose, mouth and whiskers.

3
colour him in!

Erase all unwanted construction lines.

Why not draw your kawaii seal splashing about near the sea shore?

Draw your
own seal.

Kawaii chick

1 Body Wing Tail

2 Add stripes. Draw in her eyes and beak. Add some feather shapes. Draw in her feet.

3 colour her in!

1 Body Tail Wing

2 Draw in her feet. Add stripes. Draw her eyes and beak.

3 colour her in!

Erase all unwanted construction lines.

Why not draw lots of kawaii chicks cosying up together in the chicken coop?

Draw your
own chick.

Kawaii dog

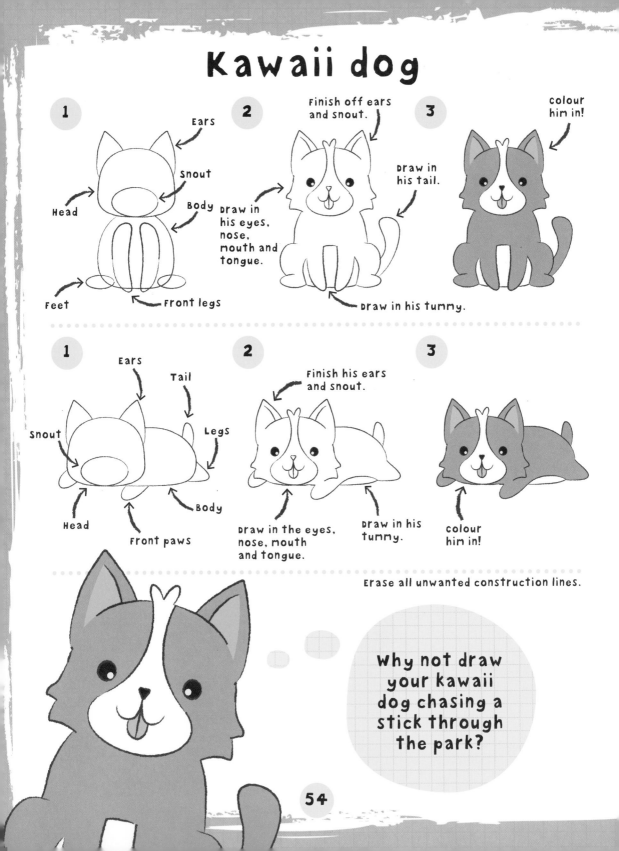

1

Ears
Snout
Head
Body
Feet
Front legs

2

Finish off ears and snout.
Draw in his eyes, nose, mouth and tongue.
Draw in his tail.
Draw in his tummy.

3

colour him in!

1

Ears
Tail
Legs
Snout
Head
Front paws
Body

2

Finish his ears and snout.
Draw in the eyes, nose, mouth and tongue.
Draw in his tummy.

3

colour him in!

Erase all unwanted construction lines.

Why not draw your kawaii dog chasing a stick through the park?

Draw your
own dog.

PATCH

Kawaii squirrel

1 Ears • Head • Tail • Acorn in paws • Feet • Body

2 Draw in her eyes, nose, mouth and teeth. • Add whiskers. • Add the acorn stem. • Draw in her tummy.

3 colour her in!

1 Tail • Head • Ears • Back leg • Body • Front legs

2 Draw in her eyes, nose, mouth and teeth. • Add whiskers. • Draw in the tummy.

3 colour her in!

Erase all unwanted construction lines.

Why not draw your kawaii squirrel up in a tree, eating her acorn?

Draw your
own squirrel.

Kawaii olm

1
Gills
Head
Arm
Legs
Tail

2
Draw in her eyes and mouth.
Add hairs to her gills.
Add detail to her tail.

3
colour her in!

1
Gills
Head
Tail
Arms
Body
Back leg

2
Draw in her eyes and mouth.
Add hairs to her gills.
Add detail to her tail.

3
colour her in!

Erase all unwanted construction lines.

Why not draw your kawaii olm swimming in an underground lake in a cave?

58

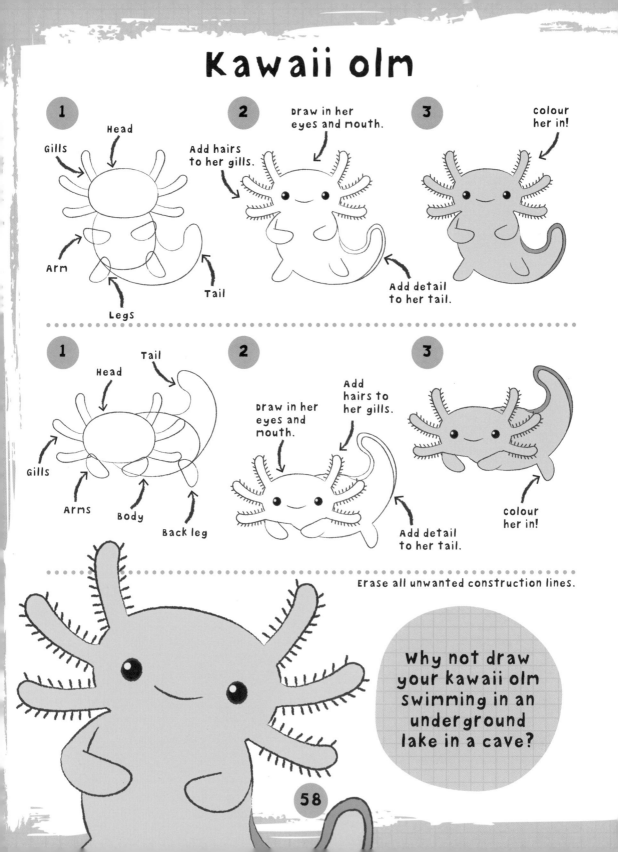

Draw your
own olm.

Kawaii otter

1

Ears

Body

Head and tummy

Feet

Tail

2 Draw in his eyes, nose, mouth and whiskers.

Finish his ears.

Draw in his tummy and arms.

Draw in his back legs.

3 colour him in!

1

Ears

Feet

Arms

Body

Tail

2 Finish his ears.

Draw in his eyes, nose, mouth and whiskers.

Draw in his tummy.

3 colour him in!

Erase all unwanted construction lines.

Why not draw your kawaii otter floating on his back in the water, relaxing?

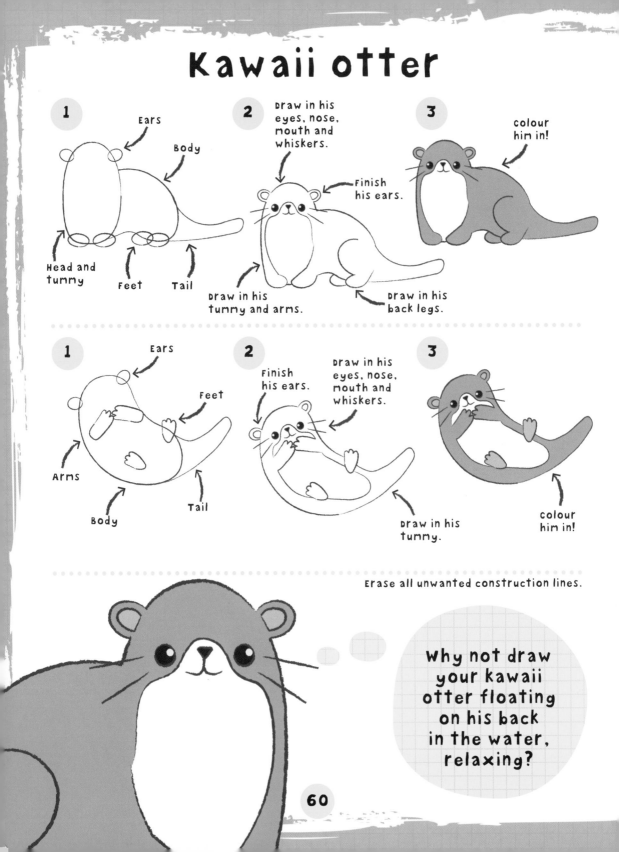

Draw
your own
otter.

Kawaii caterpillar

1

Antennae

Fat body

2

Draw a wiggly line around her body.

Draw in squiggly stripes.

Draw in her eyes, mouth and antennae.

Draw on lots of teenie, weenie feet.

3

colour her in!

1

Antennae

Head

Fat body

2

Draw in squiggly stripes.

Draw a wiggly line around her body.

Draw her eyes, mouth and antennae.

3

colour her in!

Erase all unwanted construction lines.

Why not draw your kawaii caterpillar munching her way along a leaf?

Draw your own
caterpillar.

Glossary

Antennae some insects and other species of animal have these appendages on their heads. They use them to gain sensory information about their environment.

Bamboo a type of very large, thick and woody grass.

Narwhal a species of small Arctic whale. The male has a long tusk extending in front of it.

Olm a blind salamander with white skin and external gills that can be found living in caves in south-eastern Europe.

Pastel shades of colour that are soft and gentle. Pastel colours are made with pastel crayons.

Toucan a large-billed, fruit-eating species of bird native to Central and South America.

Index